HI, IT'S ME AGAIN

T0387715

Also By Asher Perlman

Well, This Is Me: A Cartoon Collection from the New Yorker's *Asher Perlman*

HI, IT'S ME AGAIN

A cartoon collection from the *New Yorker's*
ASHER PERLMAN

Andrews McMeel
PUBLISHING®

Hi, It's Me Again copyright © 2025 by Asher Perlman. All rights reserved. Printed in Malaysia. No part of this book may be used or reproduced in any manner whatsoever without written permission, except in the case of reprints in the context of reviews.

Andrews McMeel Publishing
a division of Andrews McMeel Universal
1130 Walnut Street, Kansas City, Missouri 64106

www.andrewsmcmeel.com

Comics on pages 19, 24, 47, 53, 60, 61, 87, 105, and 124
originally appeared in the *New Yorker*.

25 26 27 28 29 TE2 10 9 8 7 6 5 4 3 2 1

ISBN: 979-8-8816-0258-1

Library of Congress Control Number: 2025933770

Editor: Patty Rice and Lucas Wetzel
Art Director: Holly Swayne
Production Editor: Elizabeth A. Garcia
Production Manager: Chadd Keim

Andrews McMeel Publishing is committed to the responsible use of natural resources and is dedicated to understanding, measuring, and reducing the impact of our products on the natural world. By choosing this product, you are supporting responsible management of the world's forests. The FSC® label means that the materials used for this product come from well-managed FSC®-certified forests, recycled materials, and other controlled sources.

ATTENTION: SCHOOLS AND BUSINESSES
Andrews McMeel books are available at quantity discounts with bulk purchase for educational, business, or sales promotional use. For information, please email the Andrews McMeel Publishing Special Sales Department: sales@andrewsmcmeel.com.

For my brothers, Reuven and Jacob.

CONTENTS

Introduction	*1*
Part One	*13*
Interlude	*95*
Part Two	*101*
Epilogue	*191*

INTRODUCTION

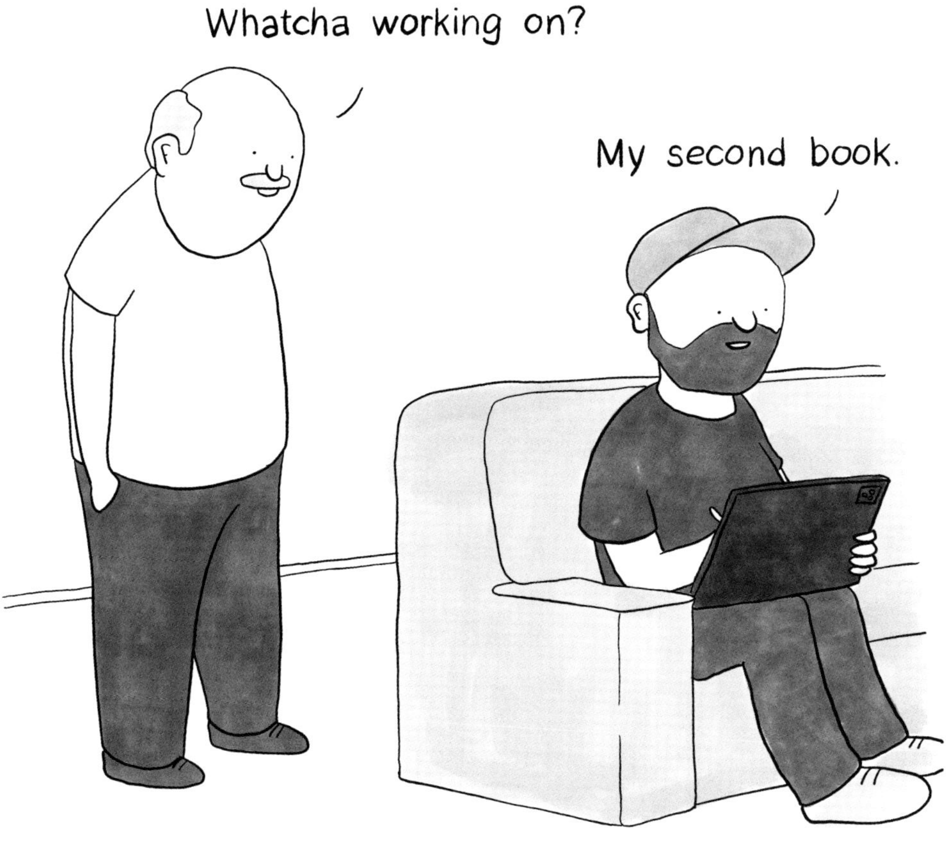
Whatcha working on?
My second book.

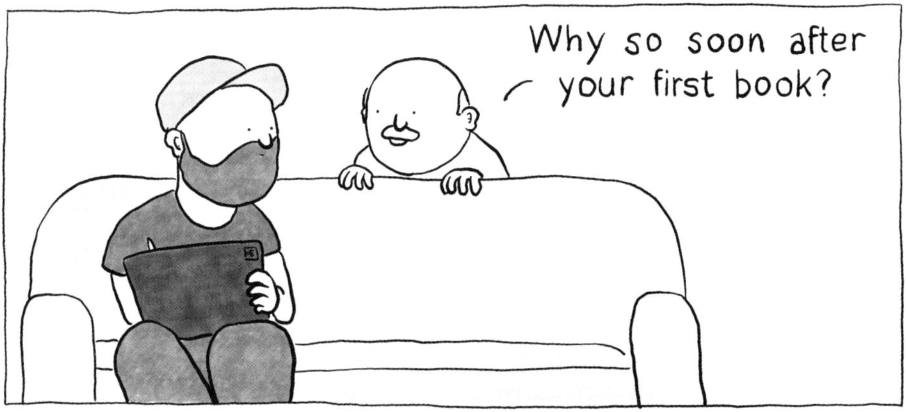
Why so soon after your first book?

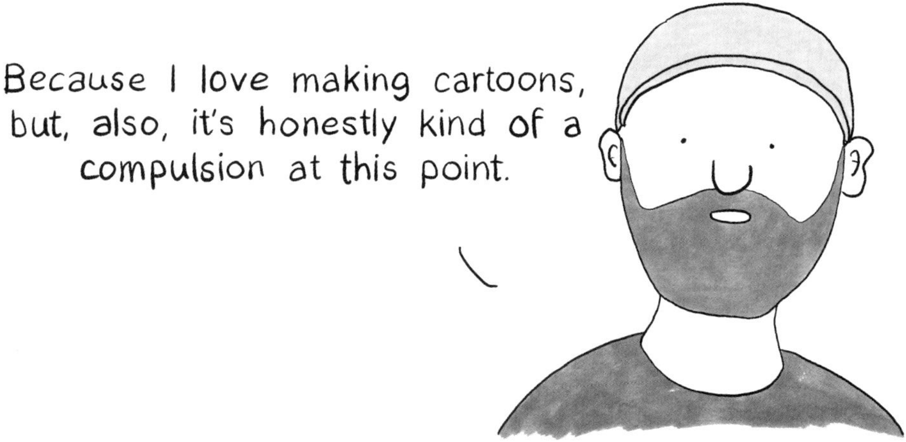
Because I love making cartoons, but, also, it's honestly kind of a compulsion at this point.

I am Sisyphus.

Except my boulder is a sketch pad.

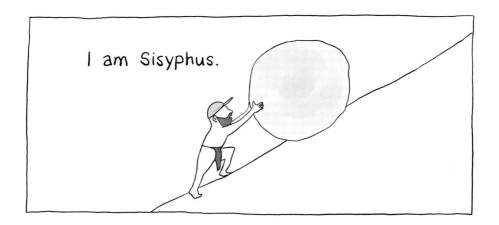

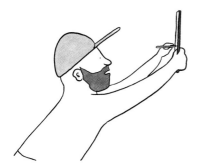

And every day, I summit creativity.

Only to tumble back
down each evening.

Where I dust myself
off and begin the
journey again.

What I'm saying is, I don't just choose to draw cartoons. I am compelled to draw cartoons.

And I'll keep making them until the day I die.

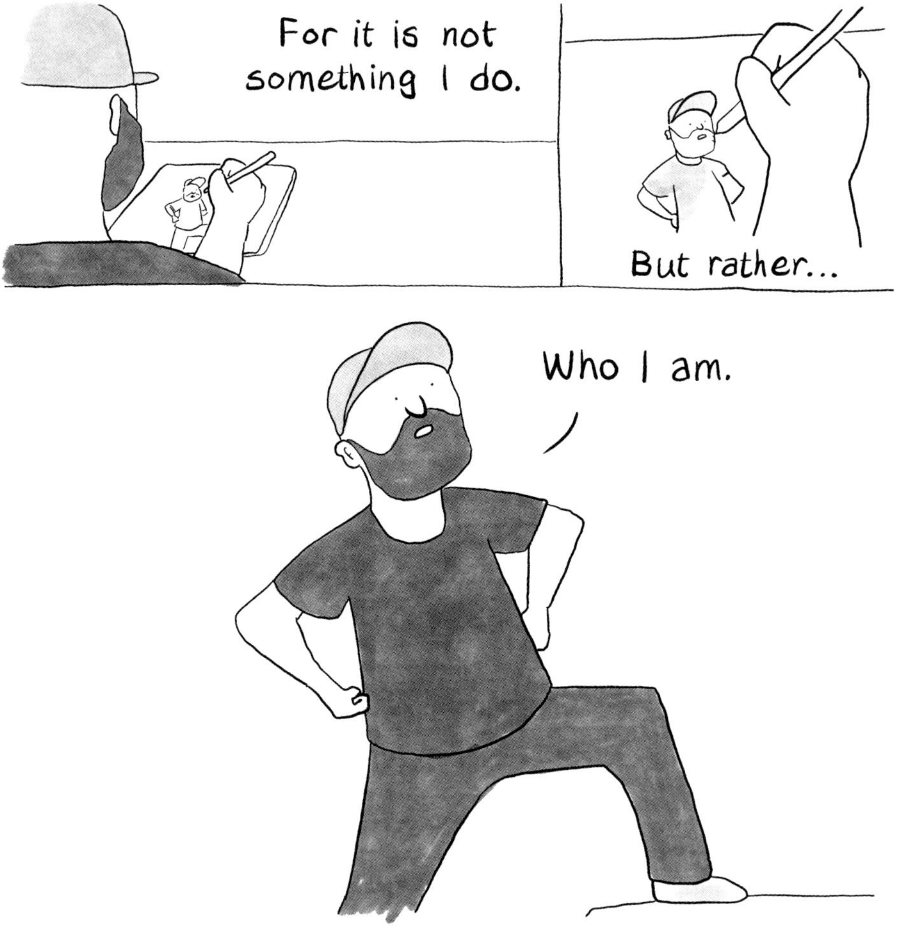
For it is not something I do.
But rather...
Who I am.

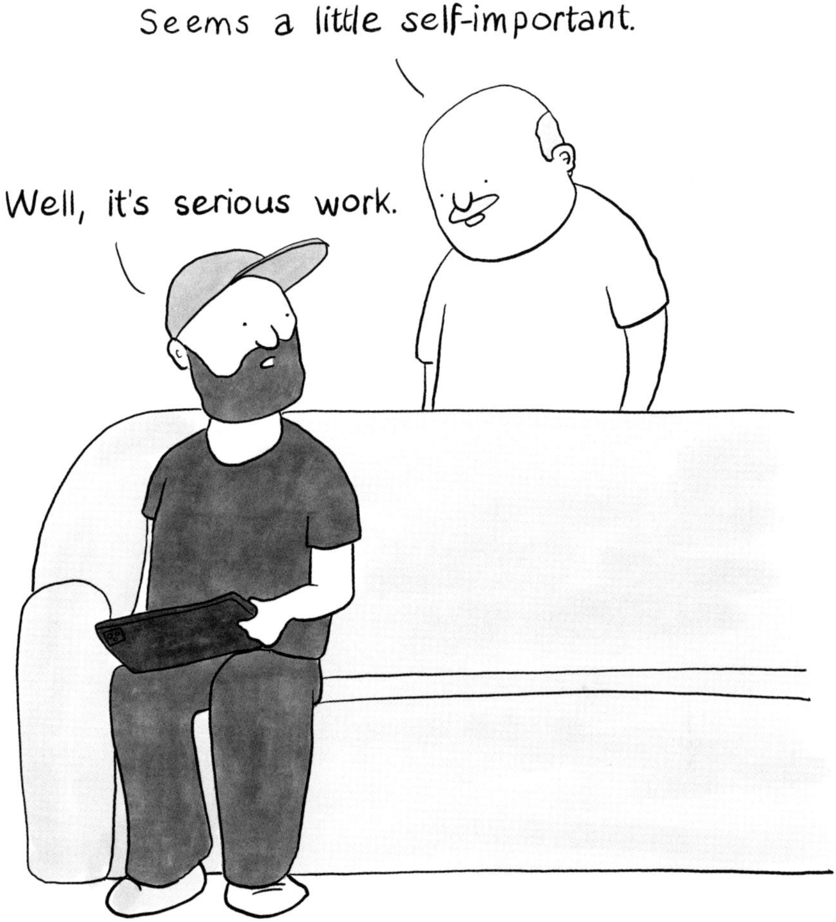
Seems a little self-important.
Well, it's serious work.

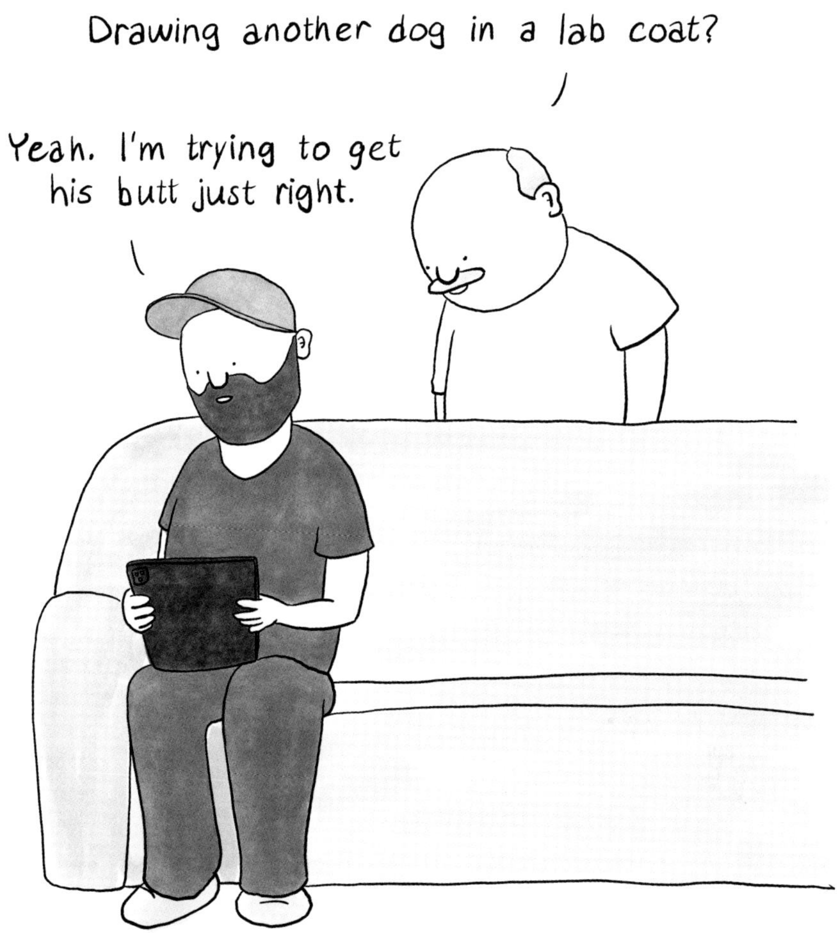
Drawing another dog in a lab coat?
Yeah. I'm trying to get his butt just right.

PART ONE

"I feel alert now, but why stop there when I can also feel sick and insane?"

"Gimme a minute. Skin-to-skin contact is so important."

"It's always so awkward to see our teacher outside of school."

"Just tell him it's sweet potato."

"We already have an internal candidate, but I didn't want to let that stop me from wasting your time."

"Latte for a guy you're sure ordered after you."

"Do what you love, and you'll see it gradually transform into an obligation, a task accomplished with the same sense of dread once reserved for what you hate."

"Sold! To the man screaming that there's a bee."

"I kinda wish he'd just use the rearview mirror."

"If you ever want to see your friends again, you must also have a baby and schedule a playdate."

"Frankly, these awards are meaningless and political, a grotesque expression of the entertainment industry's inherent narcissism. Unless I win."

"Your honor, may I approach the bench and pray that I come up with something by the time I get there?"

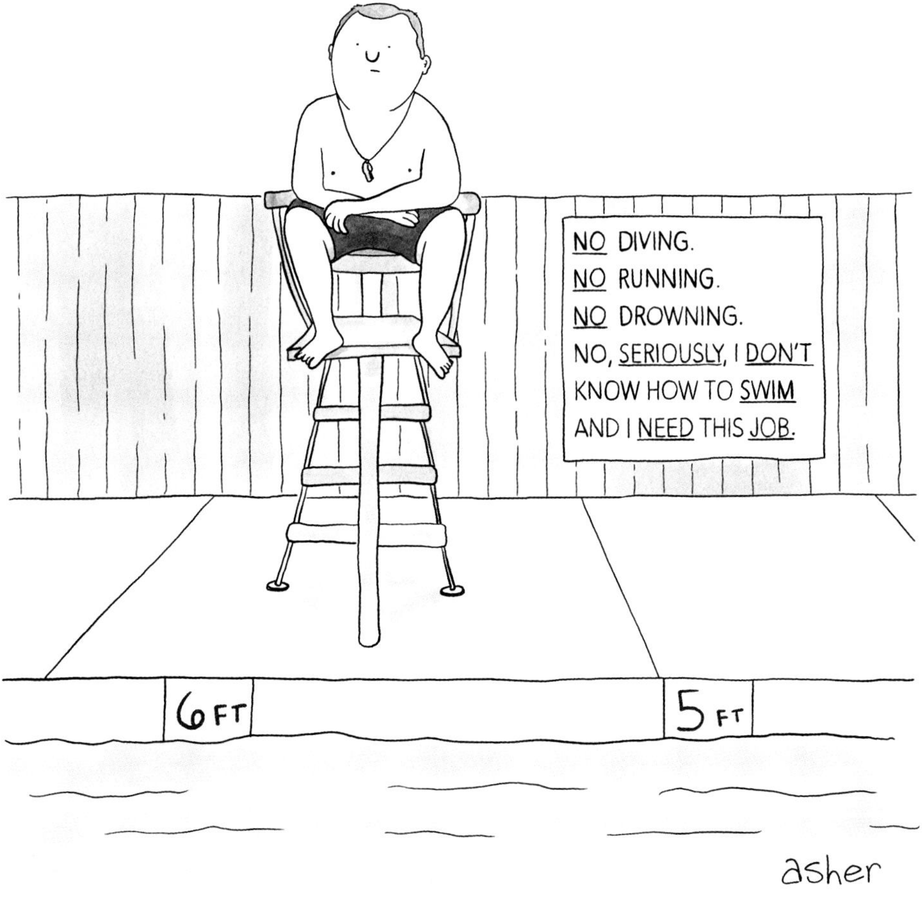
NO DIVING.
NO RUNNING.
NO DROWNING.
NO, SERIOUSLY, I DON'T KNOW HOW TO SWIM AND I NEED THIS JOB.
6 FT
5 FT
asher

"It's just that it will be hard to fulfill your third wish if your first two are 'fuck off' and 'die.'"

"We'll call them 'hazard lights' because they will be used exclusively in the event of an emergency or if you wanna, like, get a milkshake or whatever."

"Thanks, but I've kinda built my entire brand around being lost at sea."

"Two houses, both alike in dignity but with dramatically different mortgage payments due to a wildly fluctuating market."

"Perhaps you'd like me to first hand over your wallet."

"Okay, biology experts uniquely positioned to appreciate the impacts of sleep deprivation on decision-making ability and fine motor skills, go forth and begin your twenty-hour shifts."

"Sorry—I can never manage to do the one thing I'm supposed to."

"I grant custody to whoever most recently peed on the child."

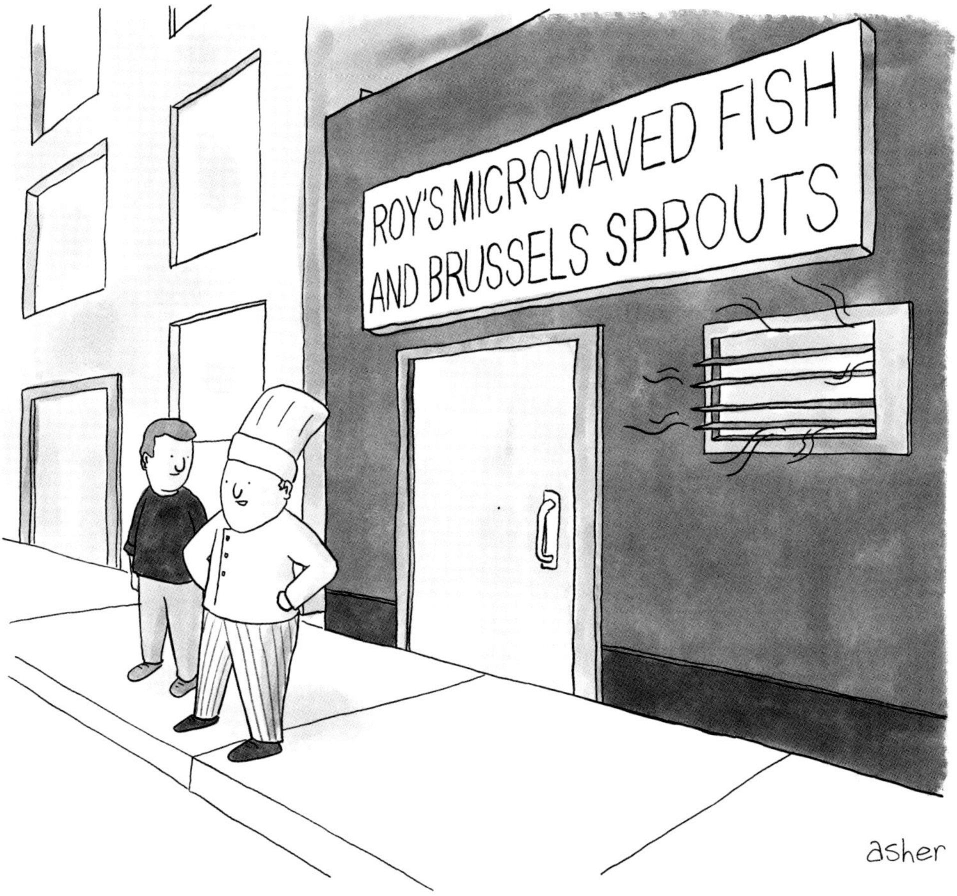
ROY'S MICROWAVED FISH
AND BRUSSELS SPROUTS
asher

"Now we wait."

"I'm working on not defining myself by my productivity."

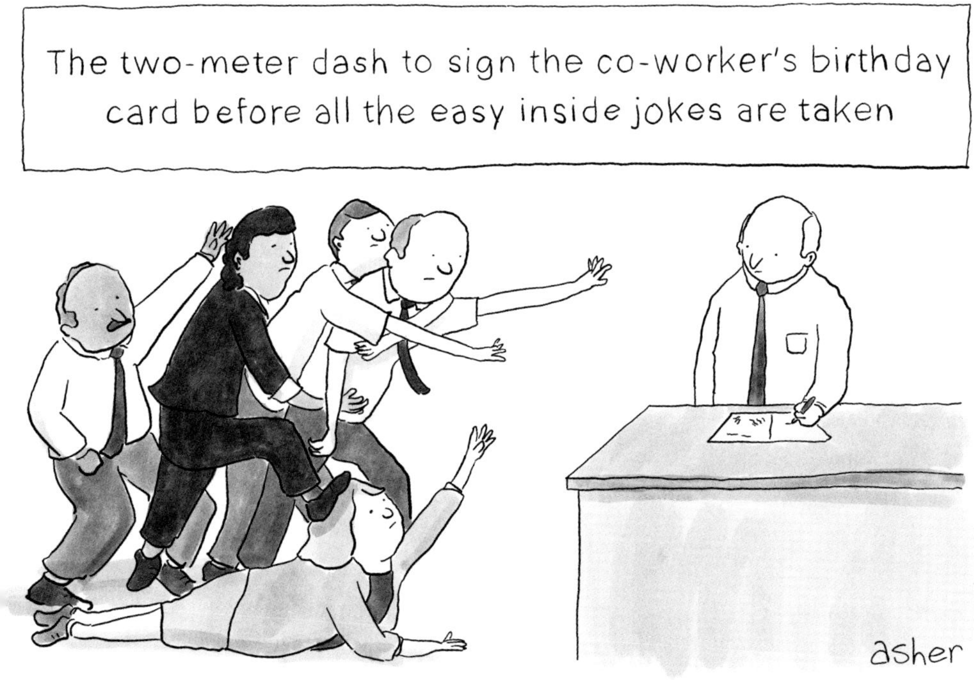
The two-meter dash to sign the co-worker's birthday card before all the easy inside jokes are taken
asher

"You need three stitches, but if you're not in a hurry,
I could do one of these lighthouse patterns."

"Sure, they worship me, but do they _like_ me?"

"Let it serve as a warning to all would-be attackers that our taste is really quite gaudy."

"Let me get this straight: I have to eat this guy's raw liver every morning for eternity, and <u>he's</u> the one who is being punished?"

"Allll you need is love, aaaand for someone with your blood type to suffer a fatal car crash in the next 48 hours that leaves their organs unhaaaarrrmed."

"I want a haircut that makes my face look like this celebrity's."

"I see a pet, but it's really more of a chore."

"Can you read this all the way to the bottom and let me know if I'm good to just sign it?"

"As a manager, my door is always open for any of you naive enough to believe that offer is sincere."

"I got into medicine because I have a passion for confirming people's birthdays."

"Actually, I'm not a firefighter."

"When I told you to write what you know, I didn't realize that everything you know is so boring."

"I'm at a pivotal crossroads where I can either continue pursuing my passion and be incredibly poor or completely sell out and still be incredibly poor."

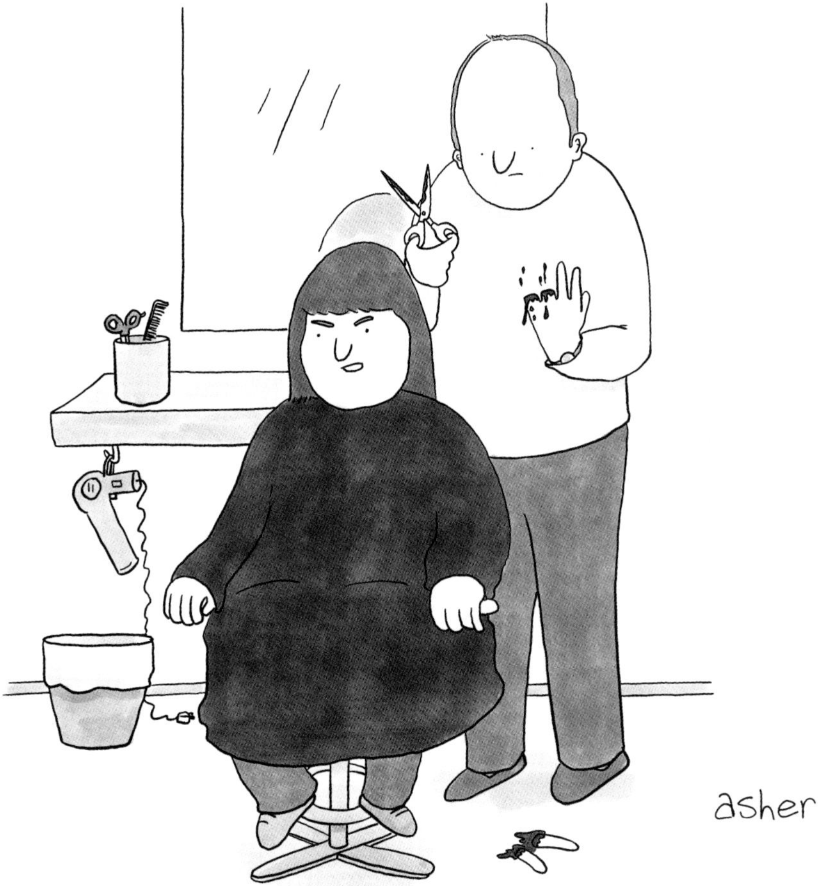
asher

"What do you mean, 'Oops'?"

"You have a clean bill of health, so you can rest easy knowing that you could still drop dead at literally any moment."

"I wasn't getting any work done at home, so I thought I'd try somewhere hot, bright, and uncomfortable."

"I have a very specific set of skills. None really apply here, but I do have them."

"There's gold in them thar teeth."

"It's just that your father and I always assumed that you would join the family business of getting tortured and beaten to death by blindfolded children."

"Please arrive 15 minutes before your appointment time, which is one and a half hours before the doctor will actually see you."

"Now, now. We mustn't give in to catastrophic thinking."

"In writing this book, I really just wanted to let people know that they aren't alone."

"And, if you think for one second that I don't deserve an acting award, just watch as I pretend to be humble."

"Wait, have you guys been hanging out without me?"

"I got us a private room so we only have to embarrass ourselves in front of people who matter, who we will see again."

"For my next trick, I will make any hope you have for getting home before 10 p.m. disappear."

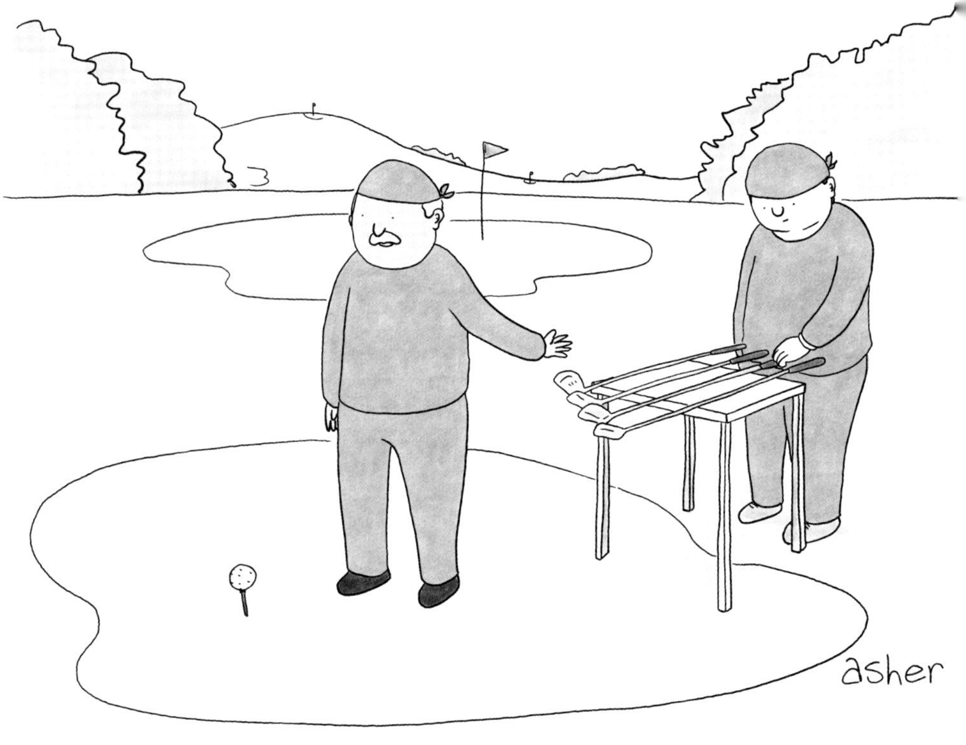
asher

"Nine iron."

"I've been eyeing his steak all night."

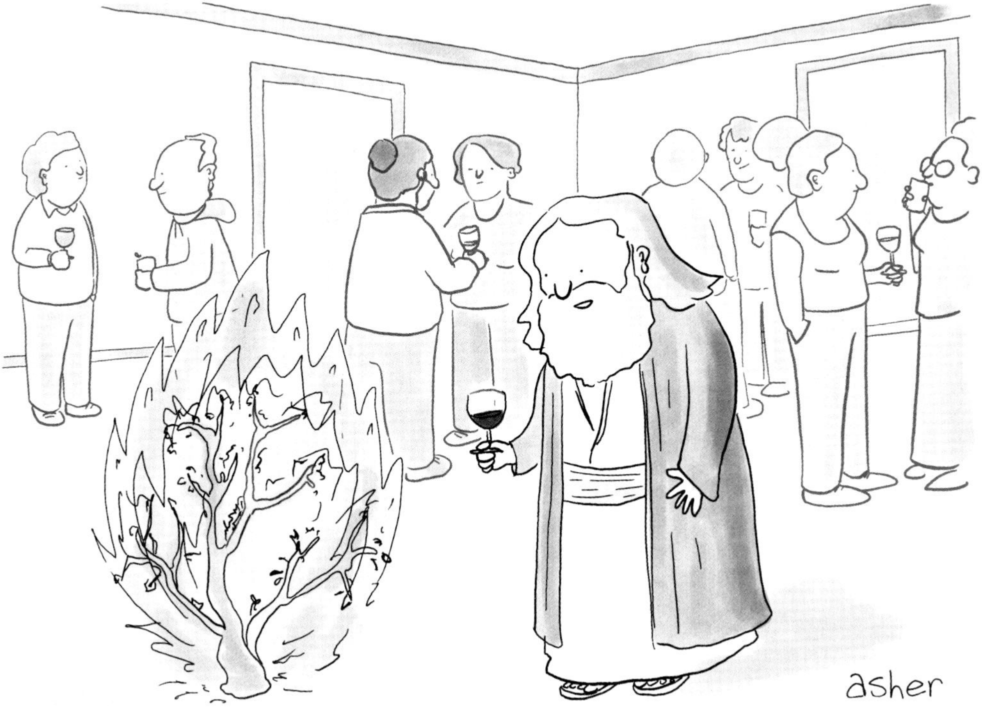
asher

"Remind me how we know each other."

"I hate to see you go, but I am truly fascinated to watch you leave."

"Ever since I successfully quit drinking, my main source of dopamine is explaining to people that I successfully quit drinking."

"Oops, you've mistaken my friendly questions for genuine interest in your job."

"Welcome aboard. We will take off as soon as the plane makes a sound that you're pretty sure planes aren't supposed to make."

"Instead of one photo of yourself that you hate, it takes four."

"Would you prefer old, dry green tea or green tea that is old and dry?"

"Your childhood bedroom was just sitting there unused, so I converted it into a home gym that also goes unused."

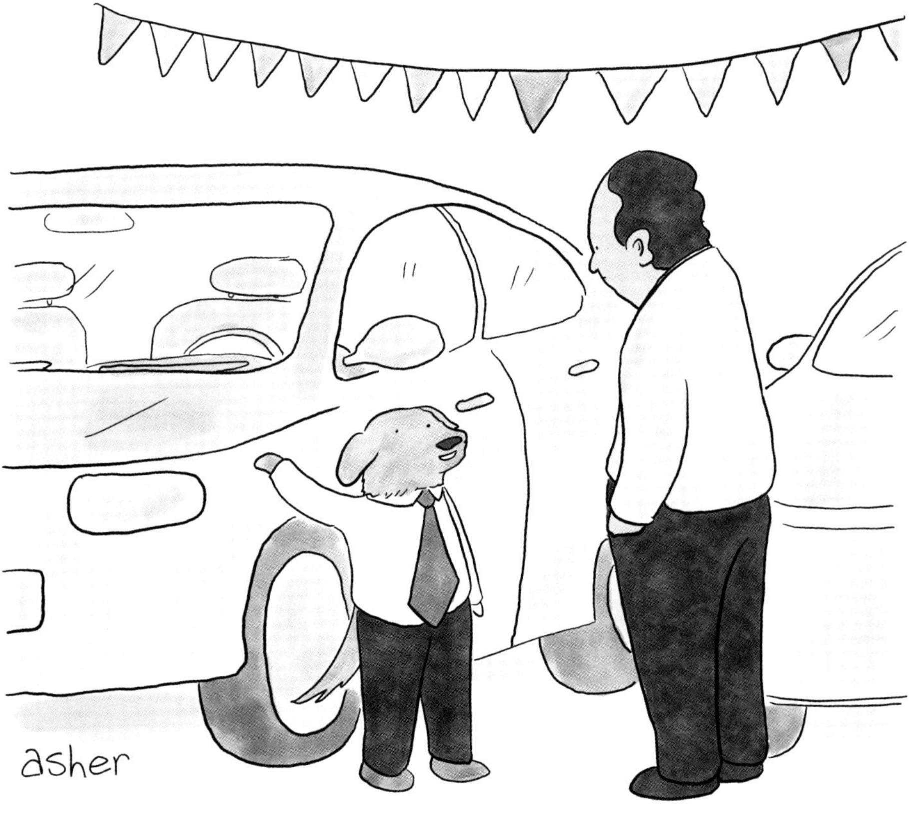
asher

"What's it gonna take to get you into this brand-new Cadillac with me in the passenger seat, windows down?"

"I don't think you want me to bring my partner in here. He's one of those guys who fiddles on his guitar while you talk to him, and you can just tell he's only kind of listening."

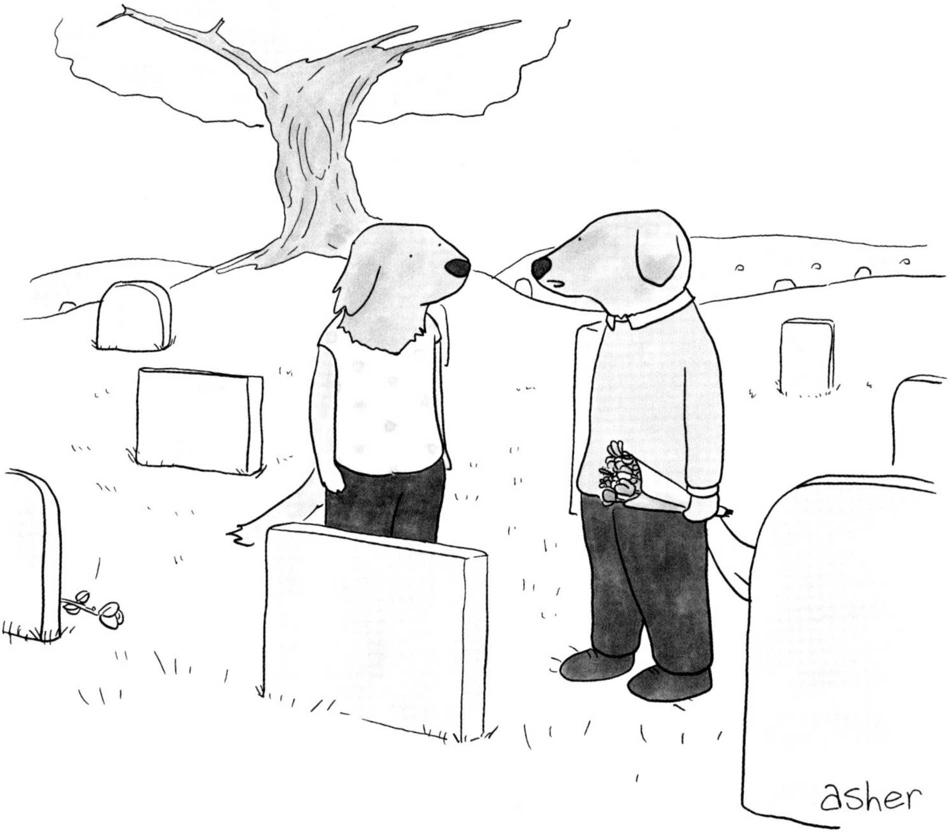
asher

"I want to dig him back up SO bad."

"Just a heads-up: if he tells you to 'roast him' and that he can 'take it,' no, he can't."

"Yes, I have a light, but only if you're willing to get pretty intimate."

"You better have a real cake in there."

"Sorry, can you tell me your name again so I can somehow miss it a second time?"

"I'm a huge cat person, but sadly she isn't really a person cat."

"While we fix the tornado siren, we need something equally as loud, so we want you to climb up there and start sneezing."

"Forty years later and I still can't decide on my first wish."

"Did we save some room this evening for a dead rat I found?"

"I don't really vant to suck your blood—I just eat when I'm bored."

"Our menu features cacio e pepe as well as dishes significantly worse than cacio e pepe."

"If you want to turn it off, you just pull this chain until you accidentally turn it back on."

"Oh, trust me: I feel completely naked without my watch."

"Your service was impeccable, but I was disappointed by something out of your control and I've decided to let that impact whether or not you can pay your rent."

"He always has to be the smartest person in the room."

"From The New York Times, I'm Michael Barbaro."

"The party's theme is 'clothes you don't already own.'"

"I billed my show as 'one woman,' not 'zero bats.'"

INTERLUDE

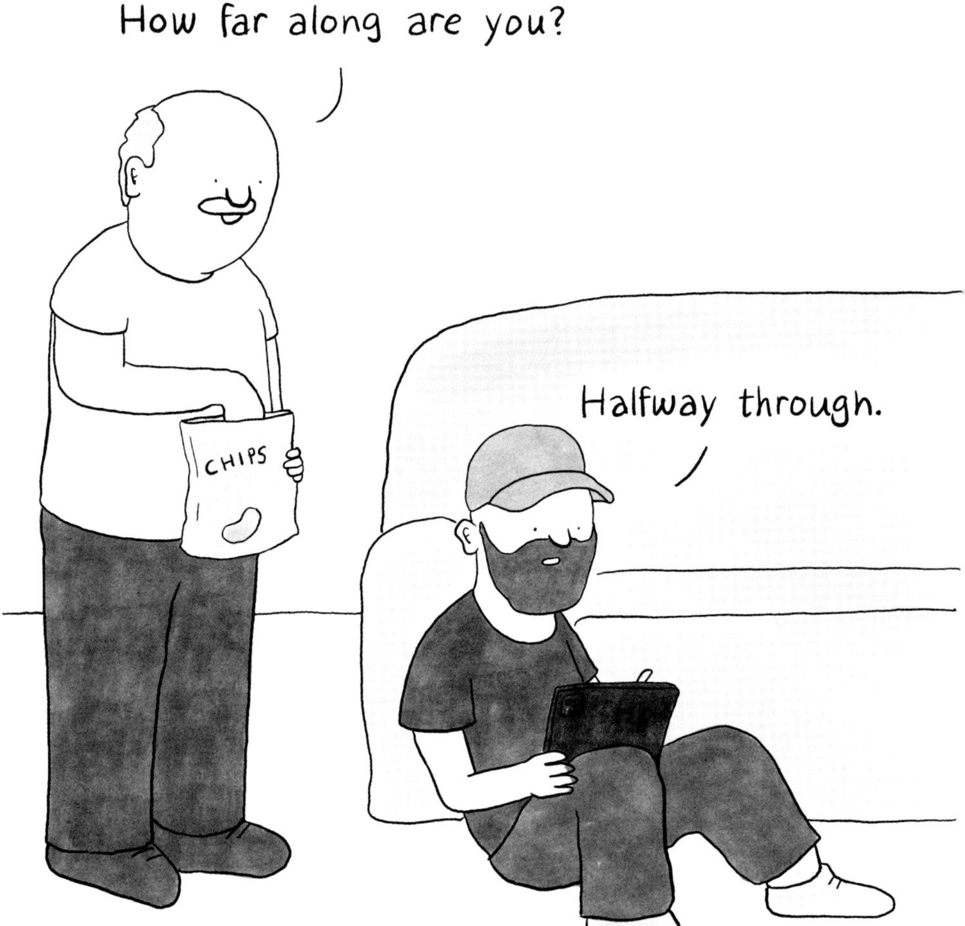
How far along are you?
CHIPS
Halfway through.

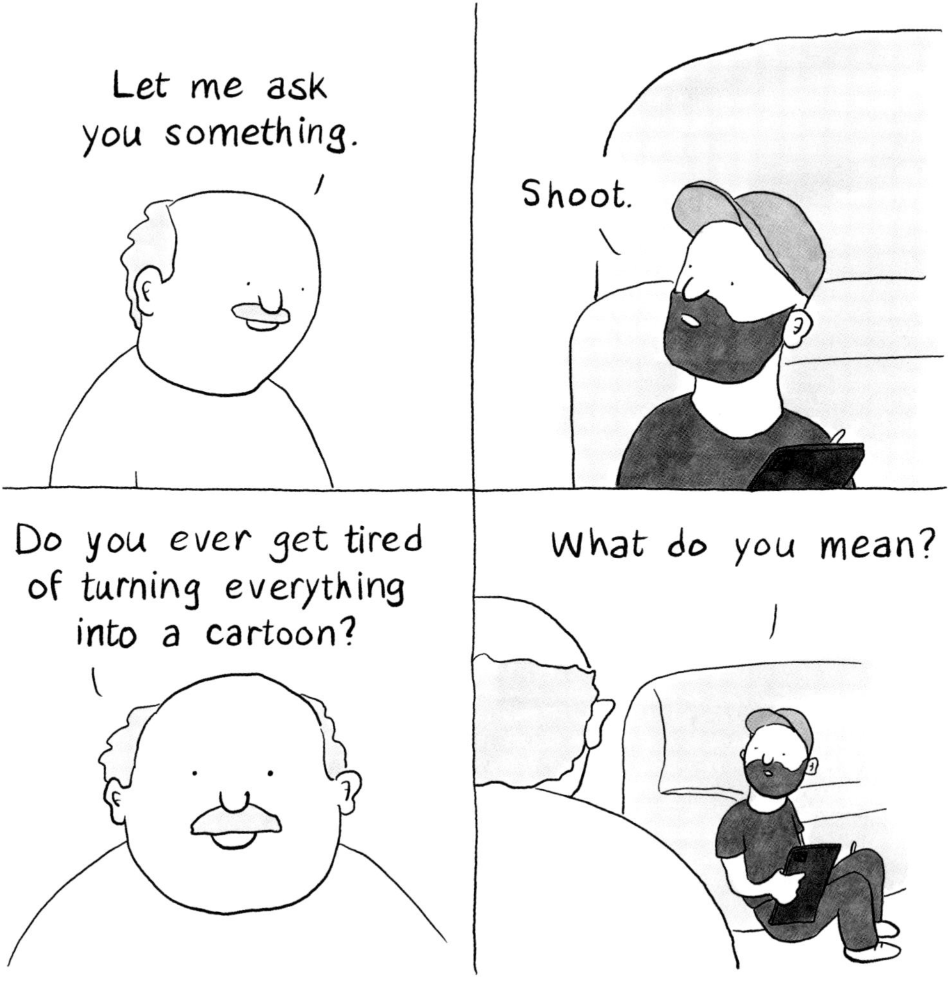
Let me ask you something.
Shoot.
Do you ever get tired of turning everything into a cartoon?
What do you mean?

Like, don't you ever just want to go about your day without the added pressure of <u>producing</u> something?

What about fun for fun's sake? Like hanging out with friends, spending time with family, playing with a dog.

If you spend your whole life turning every moment into content, doesn't that kind of rob you of the experience of actually living it?

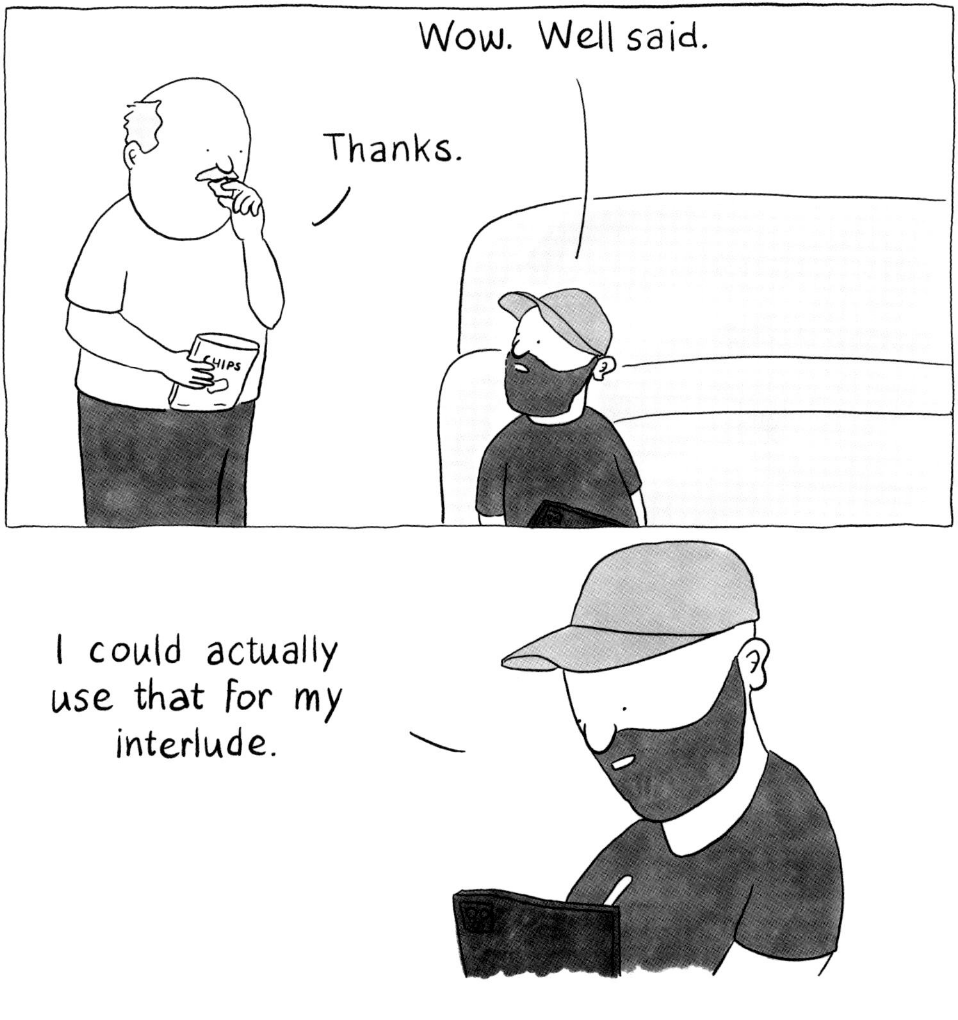
Wow. Well said.
Thanks.
CHIPS
I could actually use that for my interlude.

PART TWO

"Behold! As I transform your harmless small talk into a reckless exploration of my insecurities."

"Having your friends help you move is a great deal because it saves you a few hundred bucks and all it costs you is the friendship."

"This is my first cousin, twice removed, once worshiped by cultists, eternally feared by all who behold his visage."

"I'm happy to host you! Here's a spare towel and a guest room with no intuitive place to hang it."

"I'll share my gossip as soon as I've gauged how long I need to perform reluctance to make sure you don't think I'm a bad person."

"You're welcome to come to my neighborhood, but I'm also happy to pretend I'm happy to come to you."

"We're planning on having a big wedding, unless we don't end up inviting you, in which case it was an intimate ceremony with mostly family."

"I don't expect you to be perfect. I just need you to be flawed in the opposite way of my most recent ex so I can delude myself into thinking you are perfect."

"She's clearly just after his money."

"Time to sit somewhere we've definitely had sex."

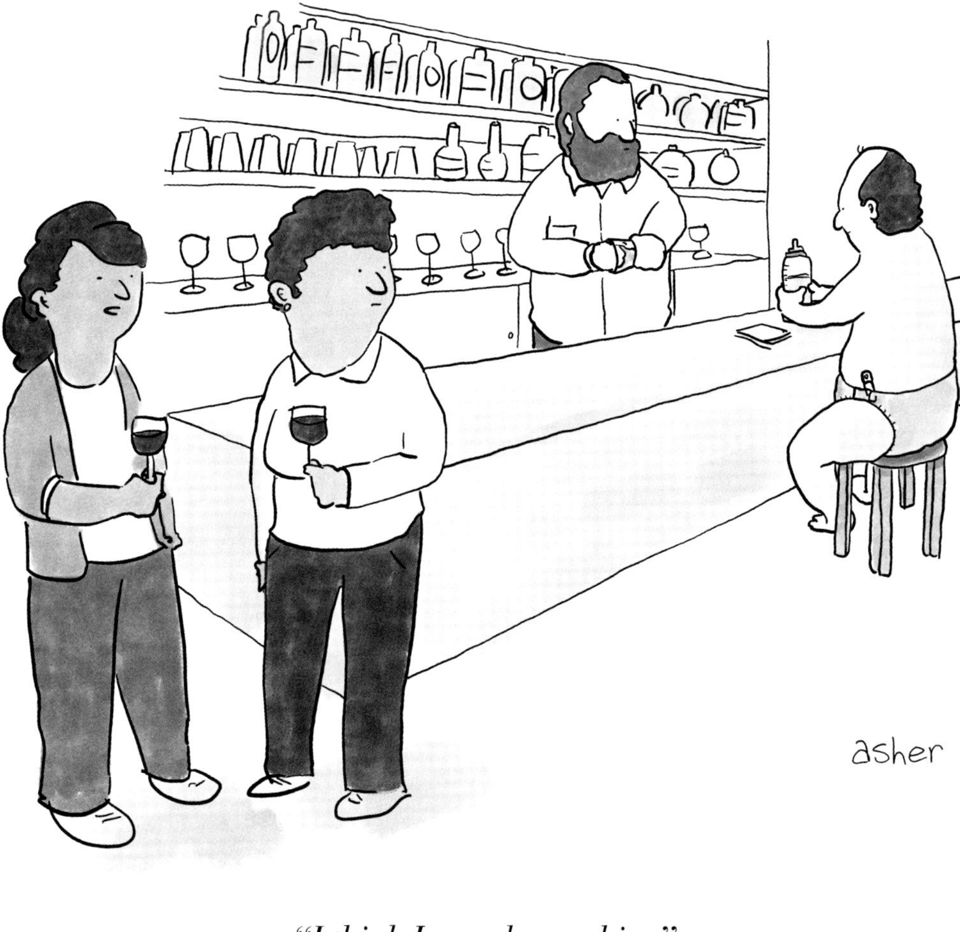
asher

"I think I can change him."

"When I suggested we role-play as strangers at a bar, I didn't mean for you to spend the entire night avoiding eye contact at all costs."

"Okay, now you tell me who's the hottest floating mask guy in all the land."

"Today, I marry my best friend."

"I hate holding hands in public."

"Your mom's diary, chapter seven: 'I'm starting to suspect that my husband is a real weird guy.'"

"Actually, you're <u>nauseated</u>. It is my <u>presence</u> that is nauseous."

"Wait, Grandpa, maybe dance like at least one person is watching."

"Is there anything else I can privately resent you for asking me to get?"

"Don't worry about it—my roommate's downstairs."

"So, is there a <u>mister</u> widow?"

"He must have a lot of hungry babies in there."

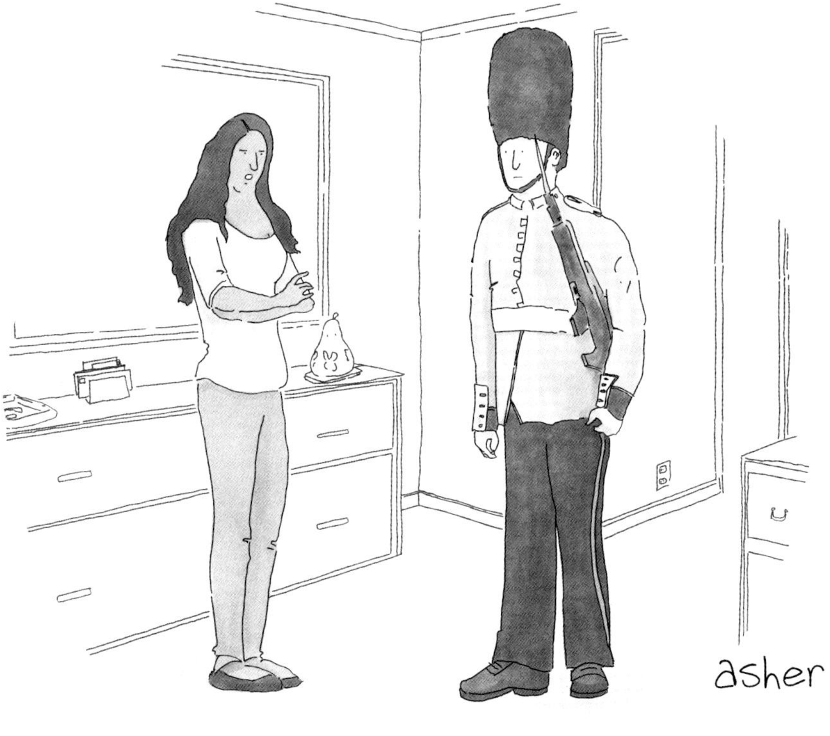
asher

"You can't just put on the uniform whenever you don't want to have a conversation, Barry."

"Please follow me to the tiny table you've been dreading would be yours ever since you saw it get cleared."

"I'm not worried about the jealousy issues that could arise from a threesome—I just don't want to interact with a stranger."

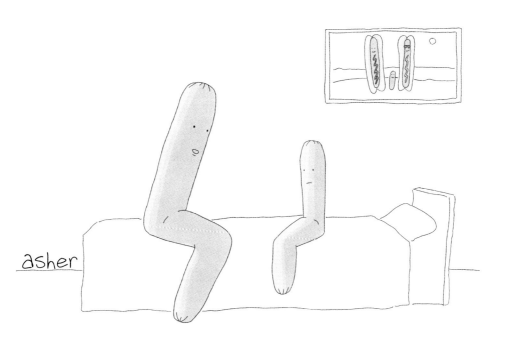

"Well, when two piles of meat really love each other, they share a special 'hug' where they are ground into a fine, homogeneous paste and combined with nitrites and skeletal meat."

"We're finally financially secure, so I say we up our spending until we're not."

"Merry Christmas! I put a bow on your car!"

"It wasn't on your registry, but don't worry: I made sure it was enormous."

"I don't know why you're so surprised. I told you, parents love me."

"Say yes, if not because you love me, because we still have 40 more minutes up here either way."

"I'm looking at Greg and Marianne's registry. Someone already got them the peanut butter, but we could get them the other peanut butter or just contribute cash to the peanut butter fund."

"Please welcome the newlyweds for their first dance as a married couple, and the groom's first in general."

"Of course I'm devastated, but I also do always love a good twist ending."

"I kinda miss the days of the kiss cam."

"I should probably have asked you this earlier: how chill are you with incest?"

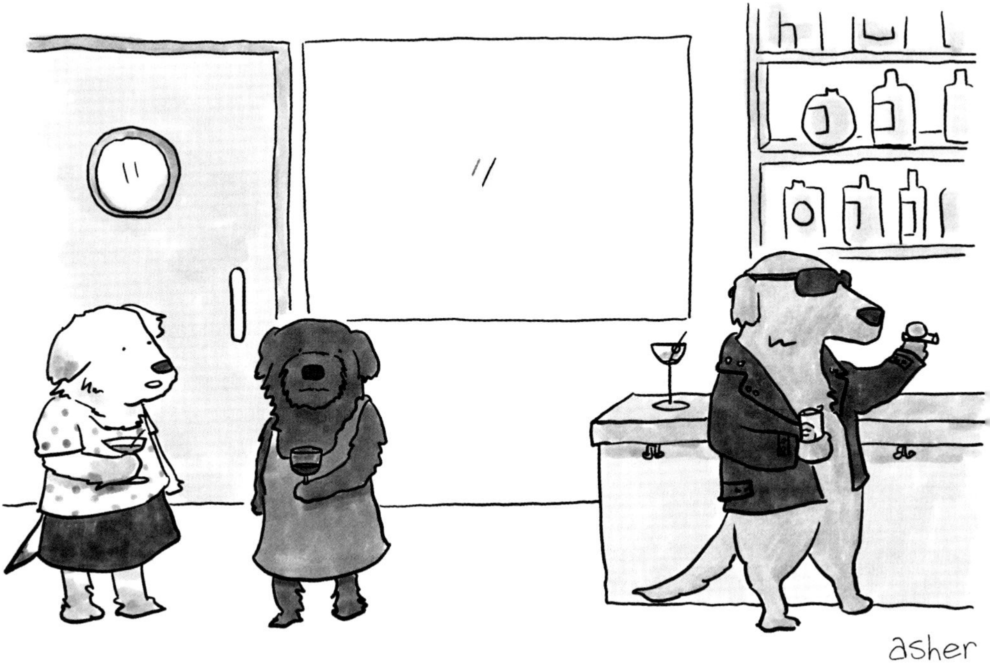
asher

"I'm tired of good boys."

"I got my tattoo in honor of the time I wanted a tattoo."

"I'm worried you're just with me for the memento mori."

"Do you rent rooms by the hour? I just need a place to shave where my wife doesn't have to see the hairs."

"Stay away! I'd rather drown than be rescued by a hot teen in front of my wife and son."

"I'm a little wiped out because I didn't get enough sleep last night or the previous thousand."

"*I like nostalgia because it simultaneously makes me wish I had appreciated the past more when it was the present and also not appreciate the present because I'm living in the past.*"

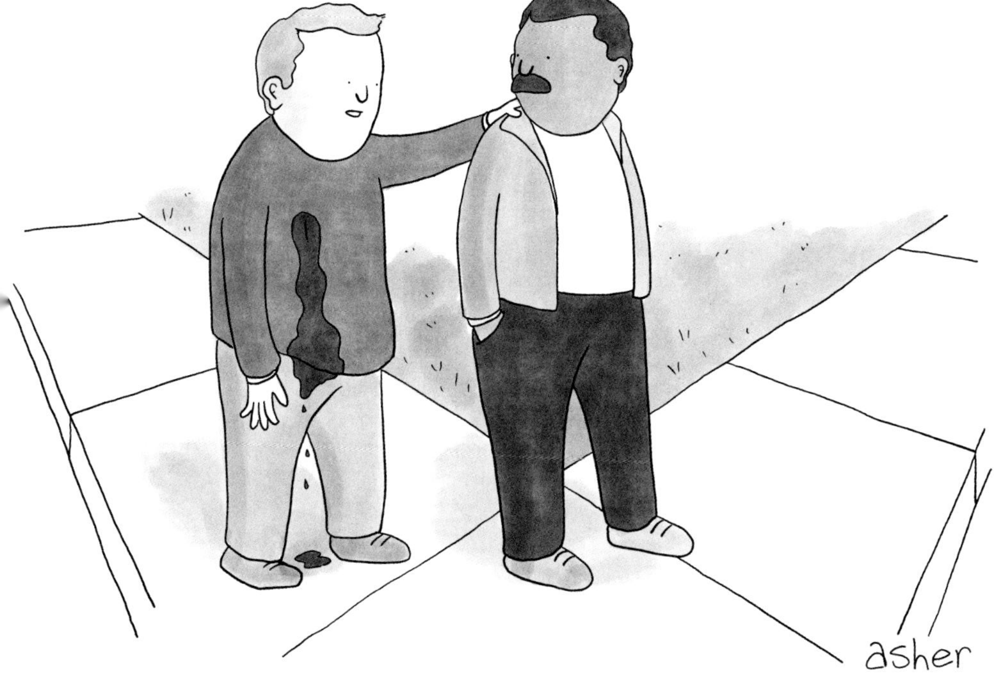
asher

"Excuse me. Sorry to bother you, but would you mind—and literally no worries if not, but if it's not too much of an inconvenience, could you possibly call 911?"

"Do you think the Snyders' house is nicer than ours?"

"Oh, what's the word? It's on the tip of my slimy tasting strip."

"I still appreciate the lost art of forcing my friends to decipher my handwriting."

"I created you in my image because I wanted someone to empathize with my chronic back pain."

"Let's just sit here and let the pressure to find the moment meaningful eliminate any chance of doing so."

"I always forget to add one ingredient."

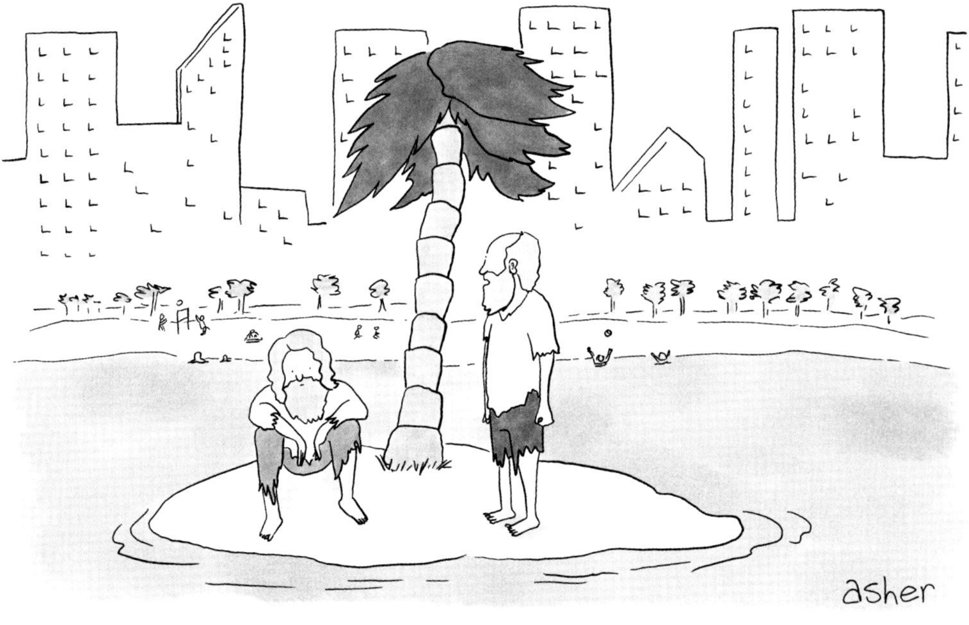
asher

"Wait, Steve, turn around."

"For anyone here for the first time, we like to start with a 10-minute warm-up that is more vigorous than any workout you've ever done in your life."

"Crashing on your couch saves me a couple hundred bucks, which I'm going to need for the physical therapy I'll require from crashing on your couch."

"Behold! As I transform this family-size frozen lasagna into a meal for one."

"I engage in too much negative self-talk, like a total fucking idiot."

"Not here, Jimmy. It ain't right."

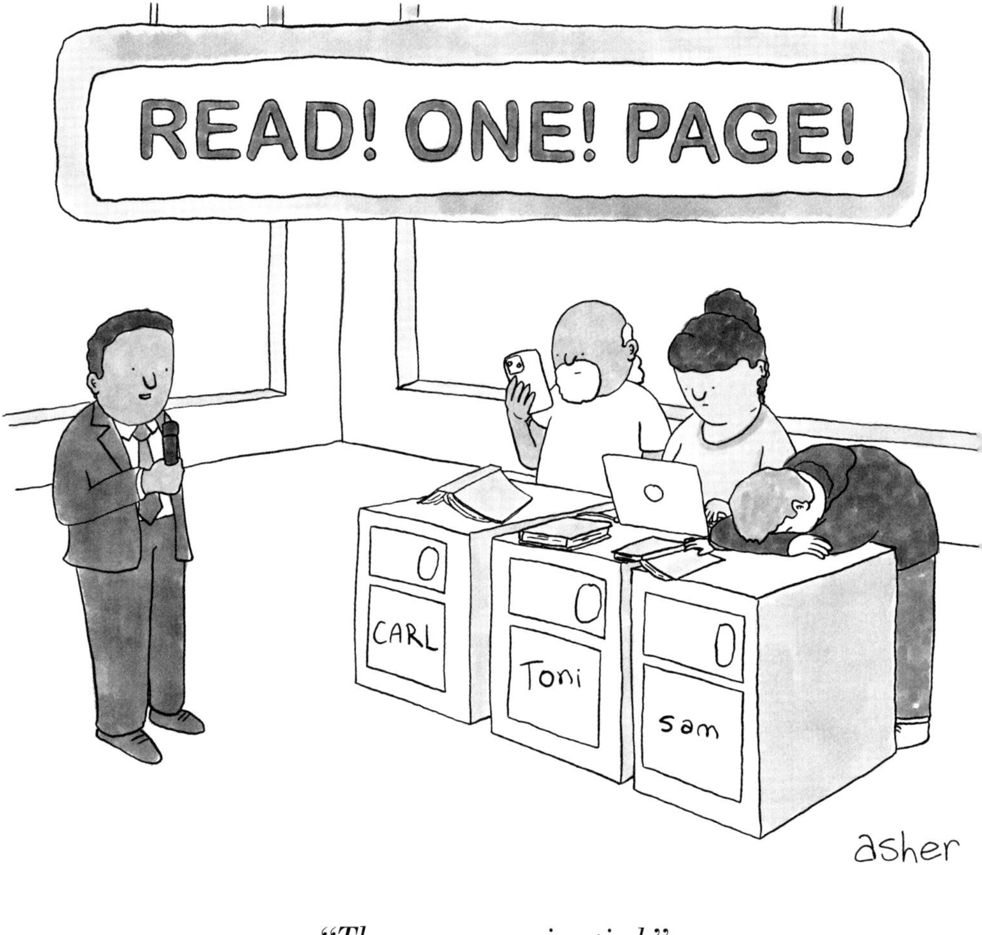
READ! ONE! PAGE!
0
CARL
0
Toni
0
sam
asher

"The score remains tied."

"Wow, I'm losing so much weight."

"I finally have all the supplies for my new hobby. All that's left now is to use them once and then abandon them forever."

"Business or pleasure ruined by spending the entire time thinking about business?"

"We all go a little nuts around the 10,000-year mark."

"I just don't understand how I could have hurt myself when I've done literally nothing to prevent it."

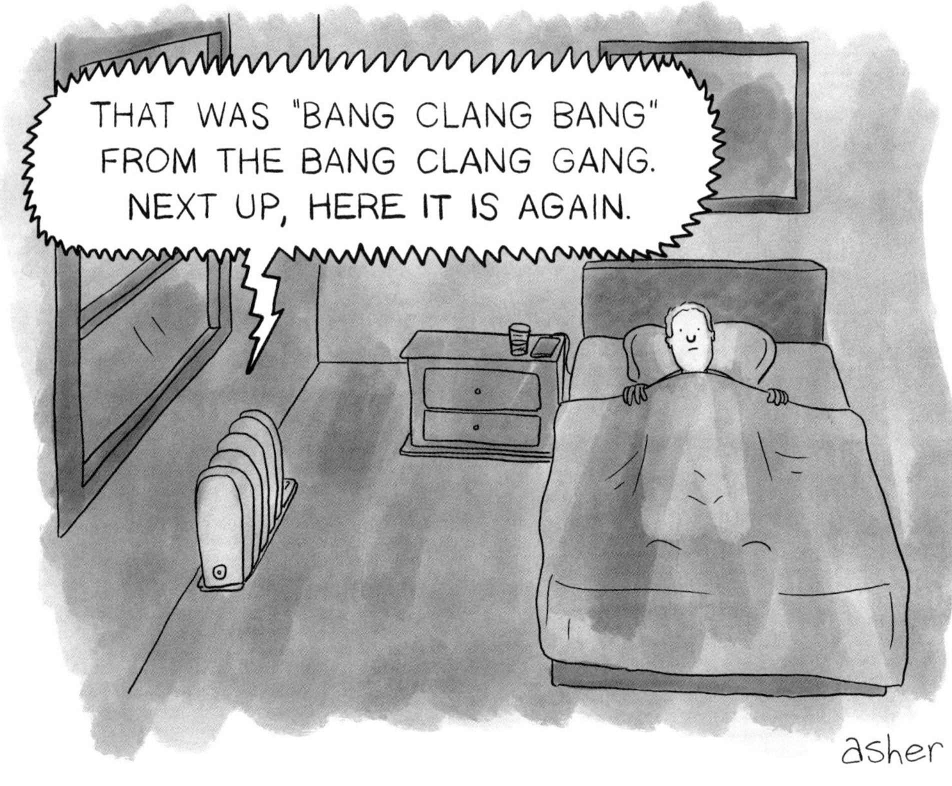
THAT WAS "BANG CLANG BANG" FROM THE BANG CLANG GANG. NEXT UP, HERE IT IS AGAIN.
asher

"One man's trash is another man."

"My unfinished business is sending one email that would take, like, 30 seconds to write."

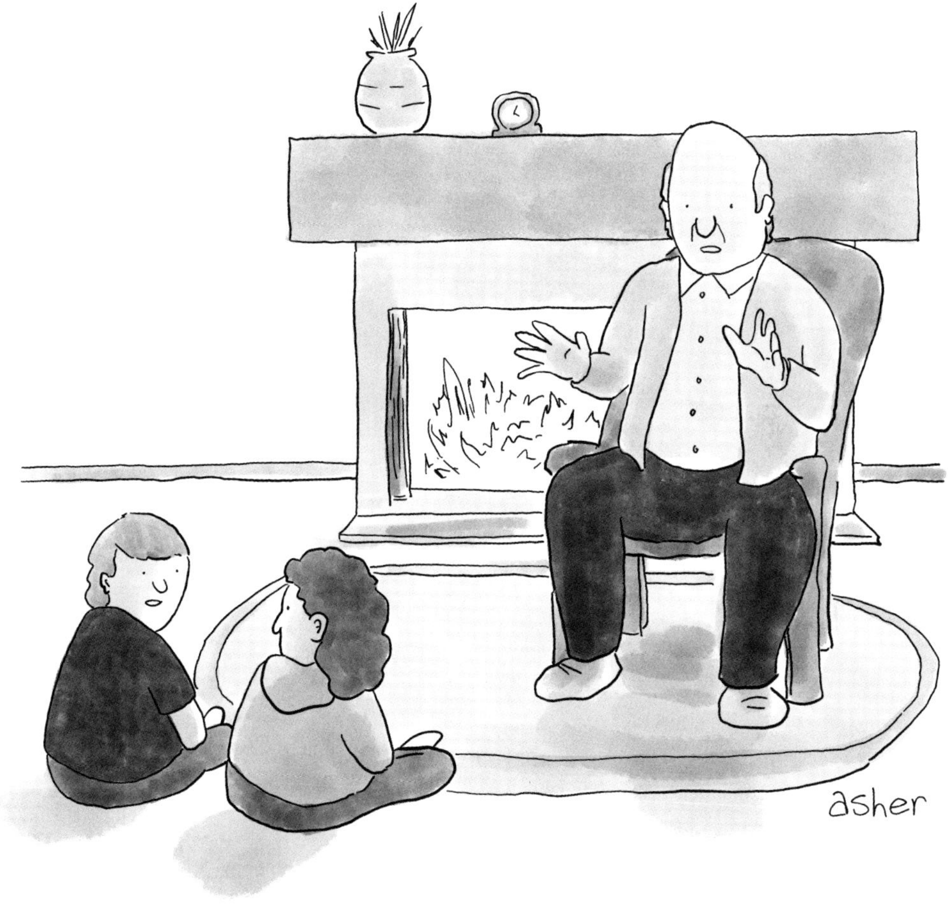
asher

"It's a rerun."

"And my thoughts would be incessant / So I'd take antidepressants / If I only had a braaaain."

"I hear you. I'm just not sure I'd judge how that went by 'number of laughs.'"

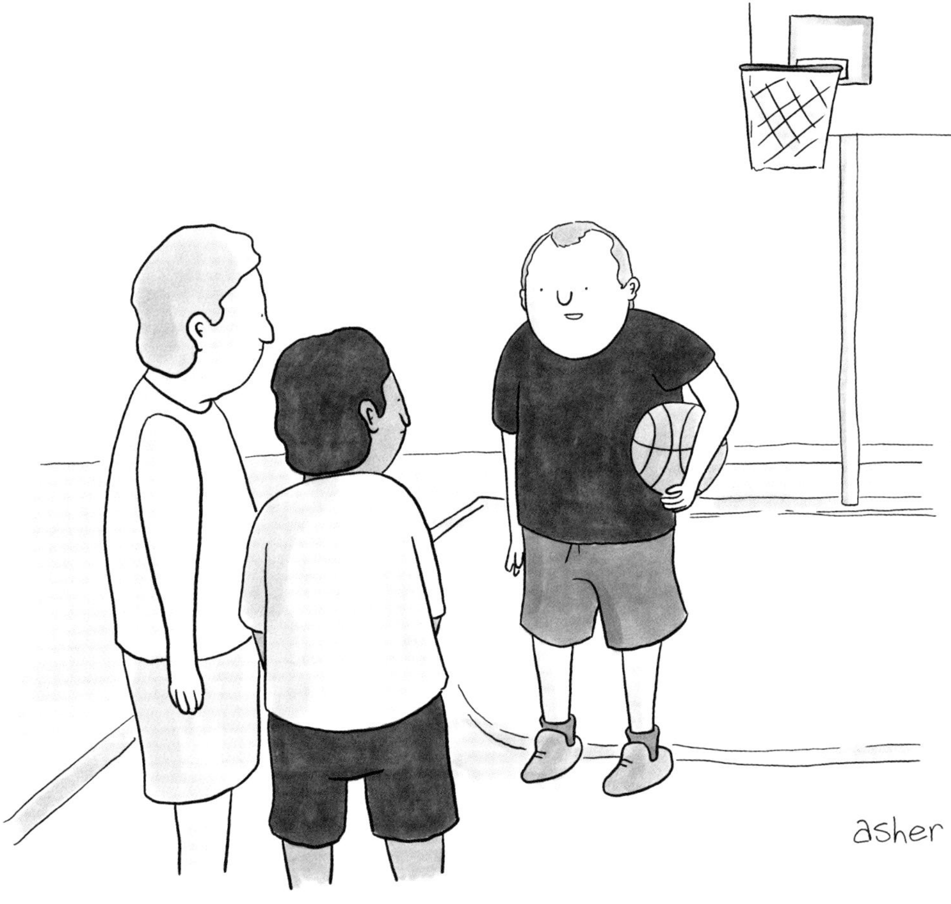
asher

"I'm between injuries."

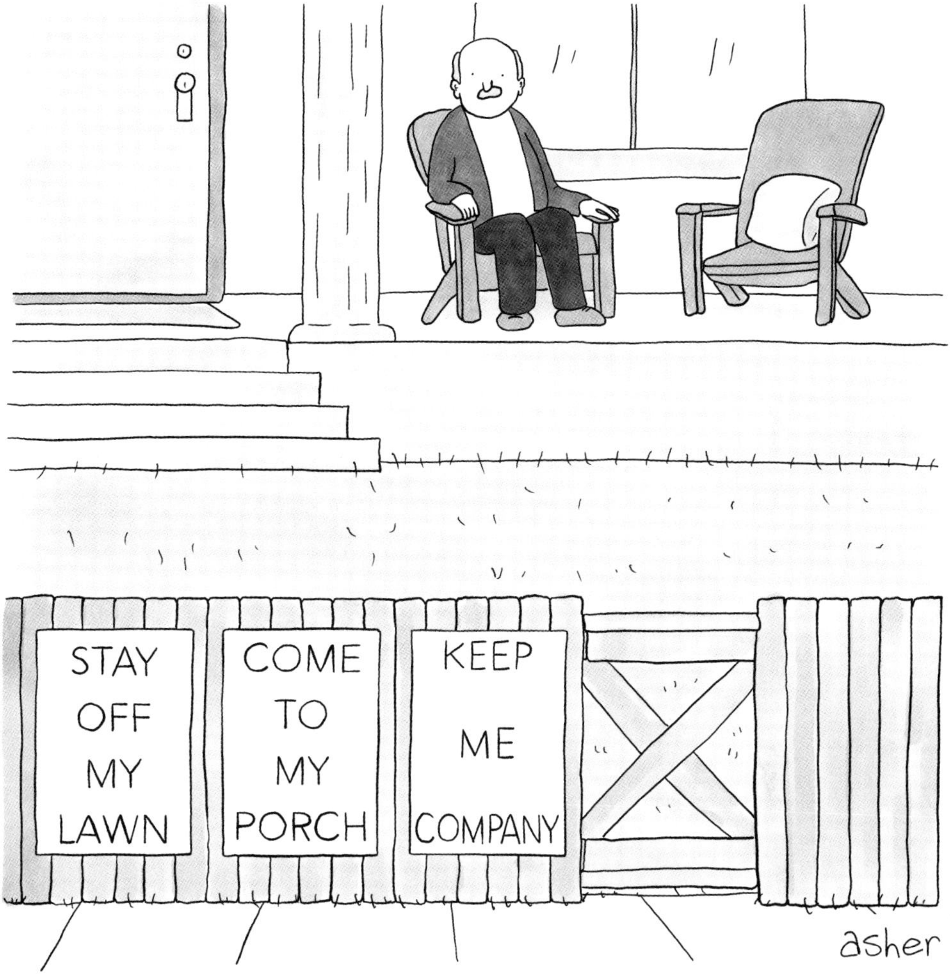
STAY OFF MY LAWN
COME TO MY PORCH
KEEP ME COMPANY
asher

"Before I go toward the light, I'm gonna bask in it for a few hours."

"If I come off as a villain, I blame the edit."

"This weekend, you should have no problem canceling plans on Friday and Saturday, but as you can see, you're probably stuck with that co-worker's barbecue."

"What I'm really running from is the knowledge that my knees are about to explode."

"I plead innocent to the charges but guilty in a more generalized sense about everything I've ever said and done."

"Let's celebrate your accomplishment by feeling like garbage tomorrow."

"Let there be more flattering light."

"Comparing yourself to others isn't so bad if you choose the right others."

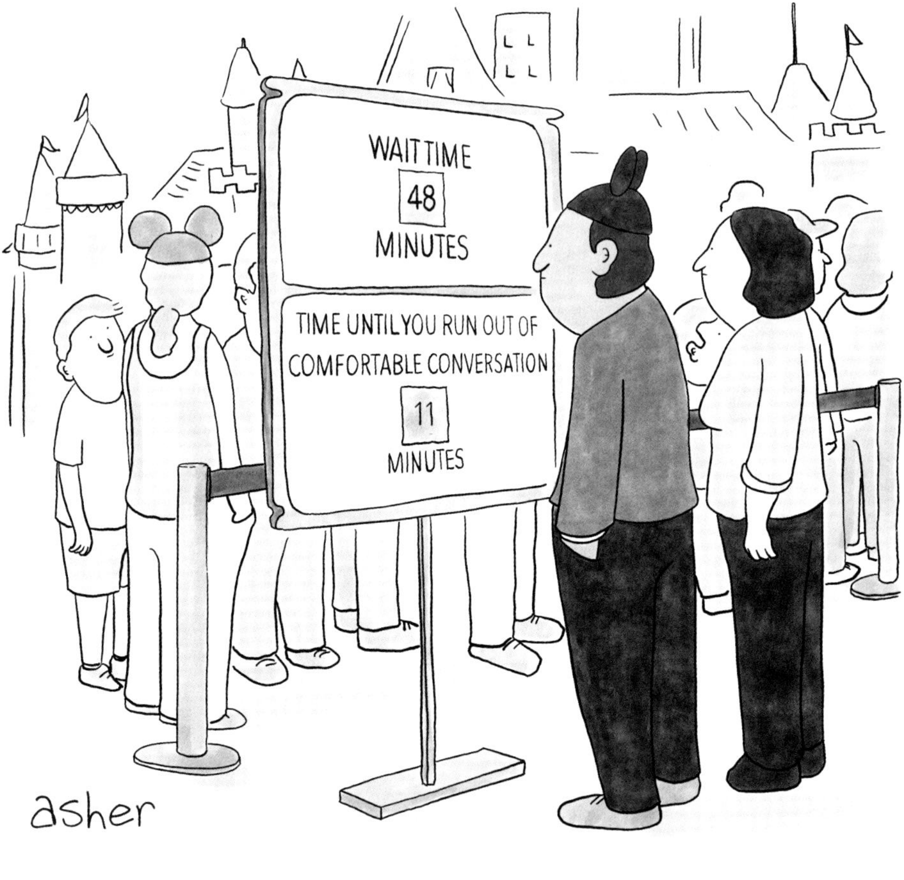
WAIT TIME
48
MINUTES
TIME UNTIL YOU RUN OUT OF
COMFORTABLE CONVERSATION
11
MINUTES
asher

"My wish is that it would be socially acceptable to scoop up all those coins."

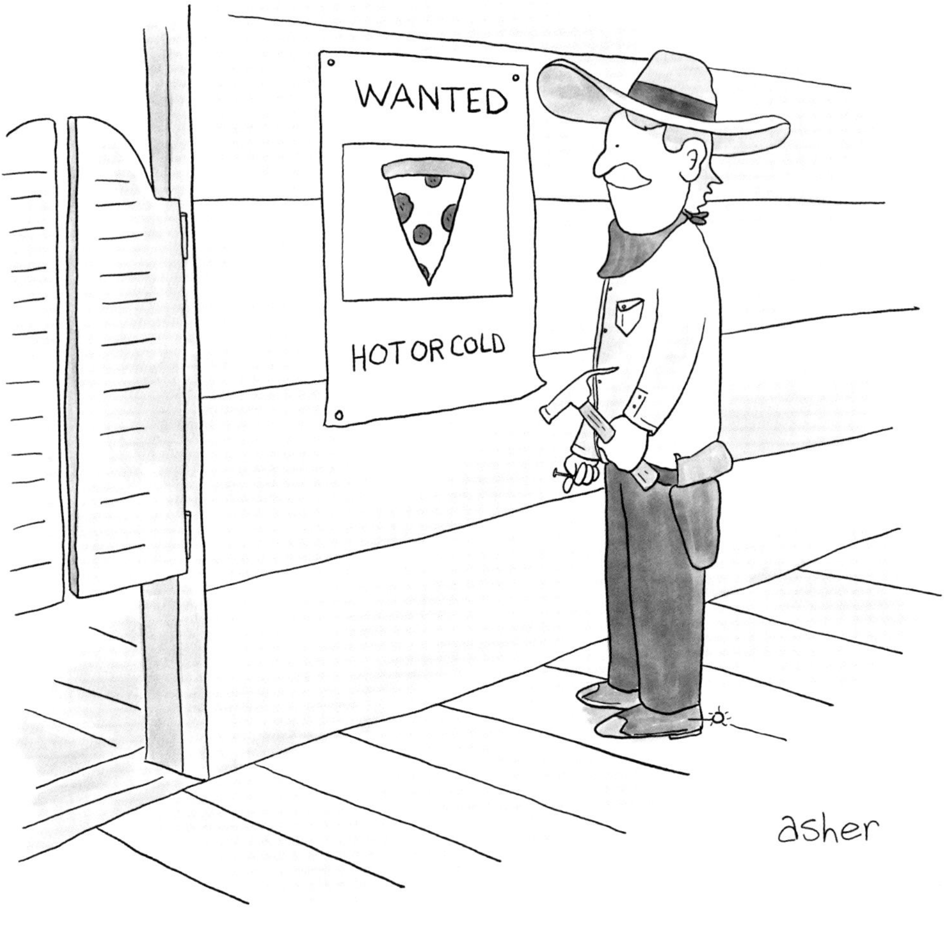
WANTED
HOT OR COLD
asher

"He's the kind of guy who would give you the shirt off his back. Unfortunately."

"I'm working on not caring so much about what other people think of me."

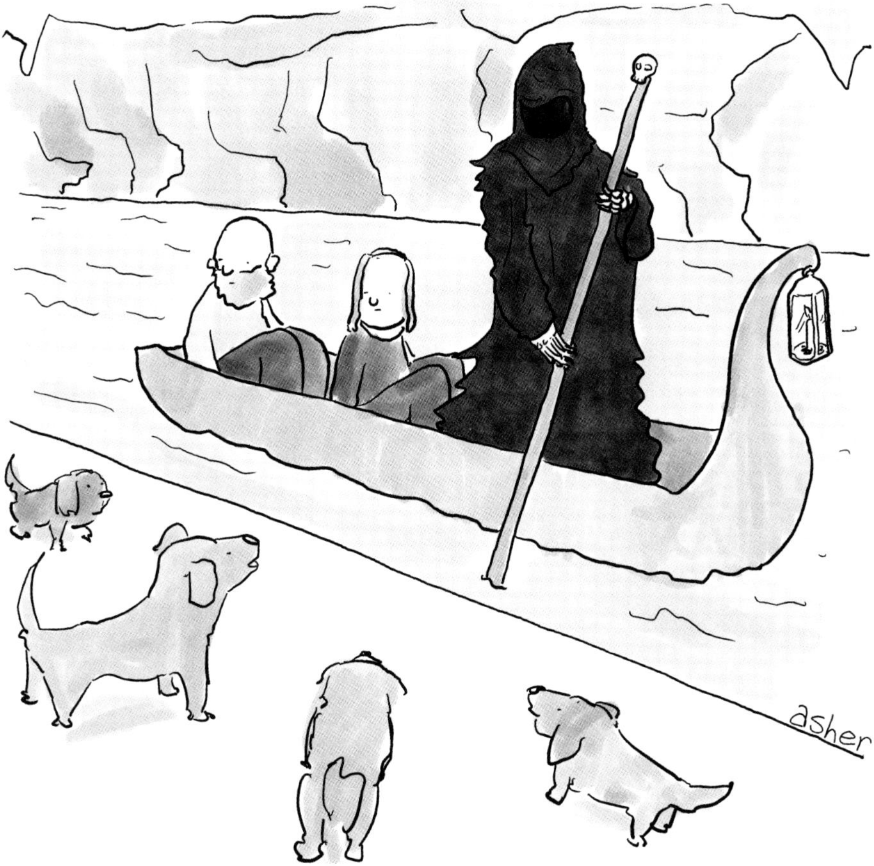
asher

"We would very much like to see this river of sticks."

"*Never give up on my dreams.*"

"I really do have an alibi, but I'm horrible at telling stories."

"Welcome to a place people generally visit for excruciatingly personal reasons. Please say out loud what brings you in today."

"He died doing what he loved: being alive."

EPILOGUE

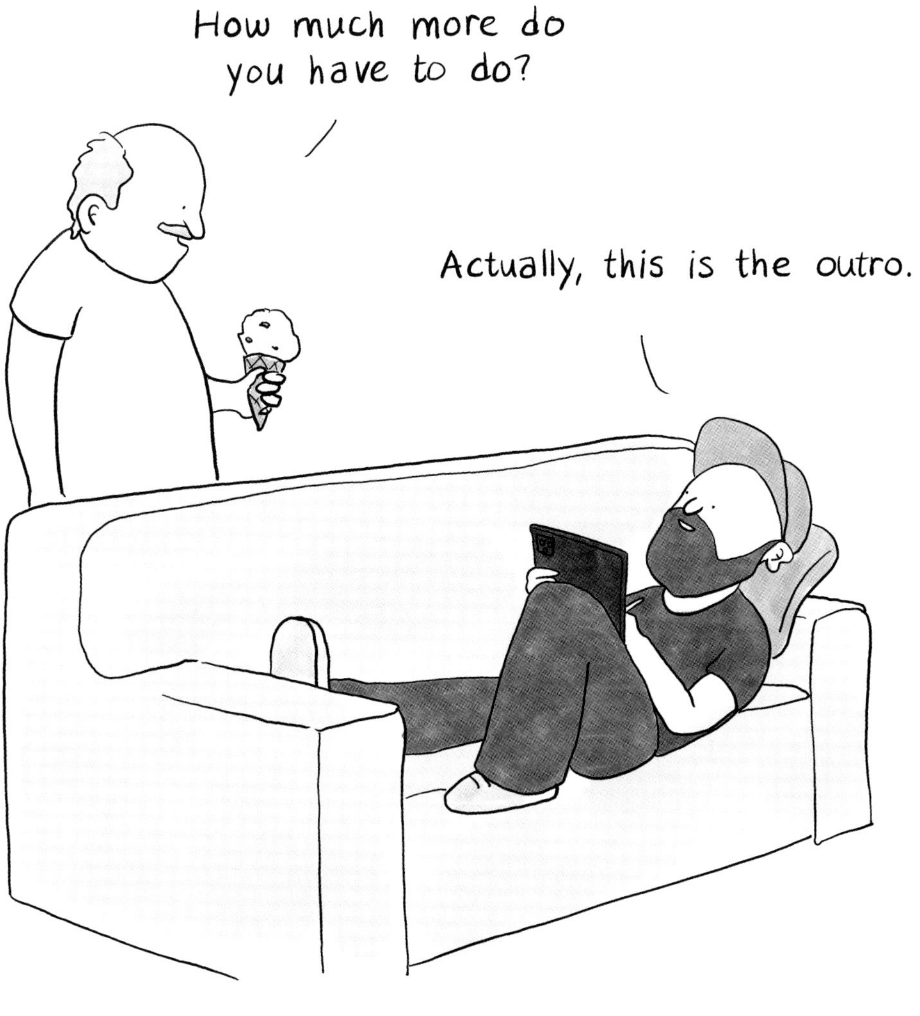
How much more do you have to do?
Actually, this is the outro.

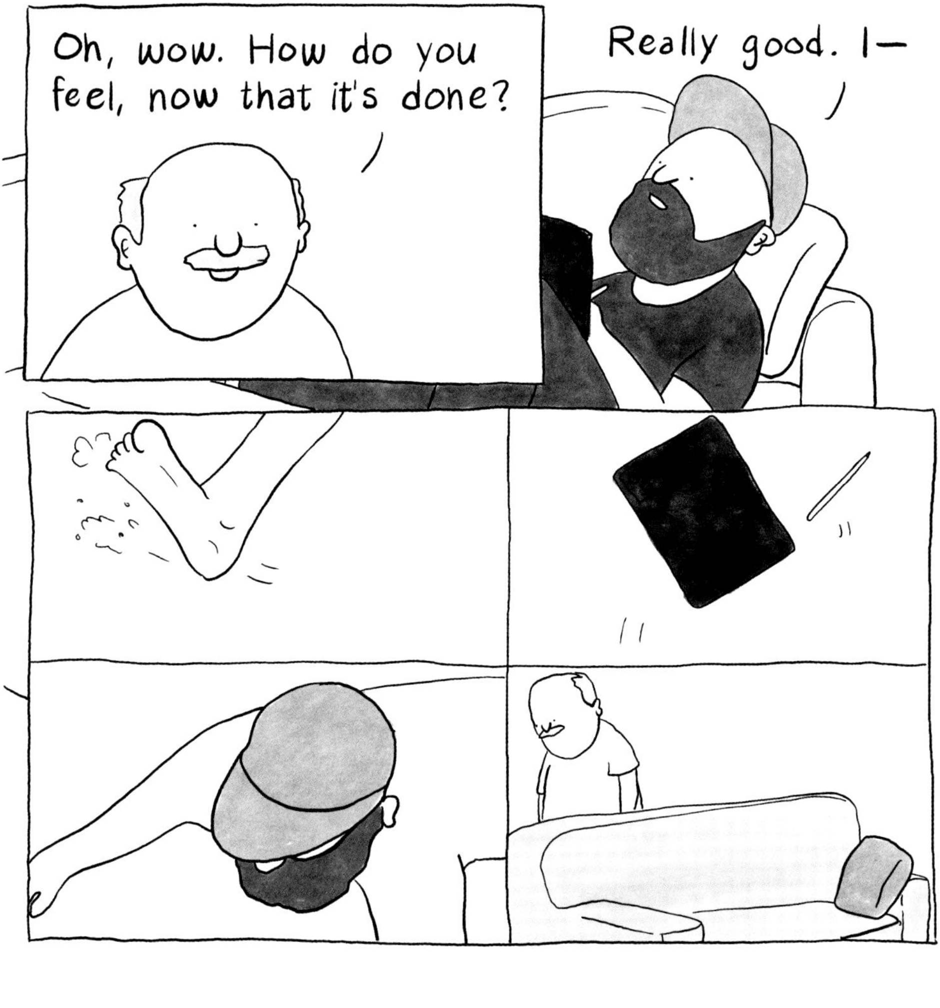
Oh, wow. How do you feel, now that it's done?
Really good. I—

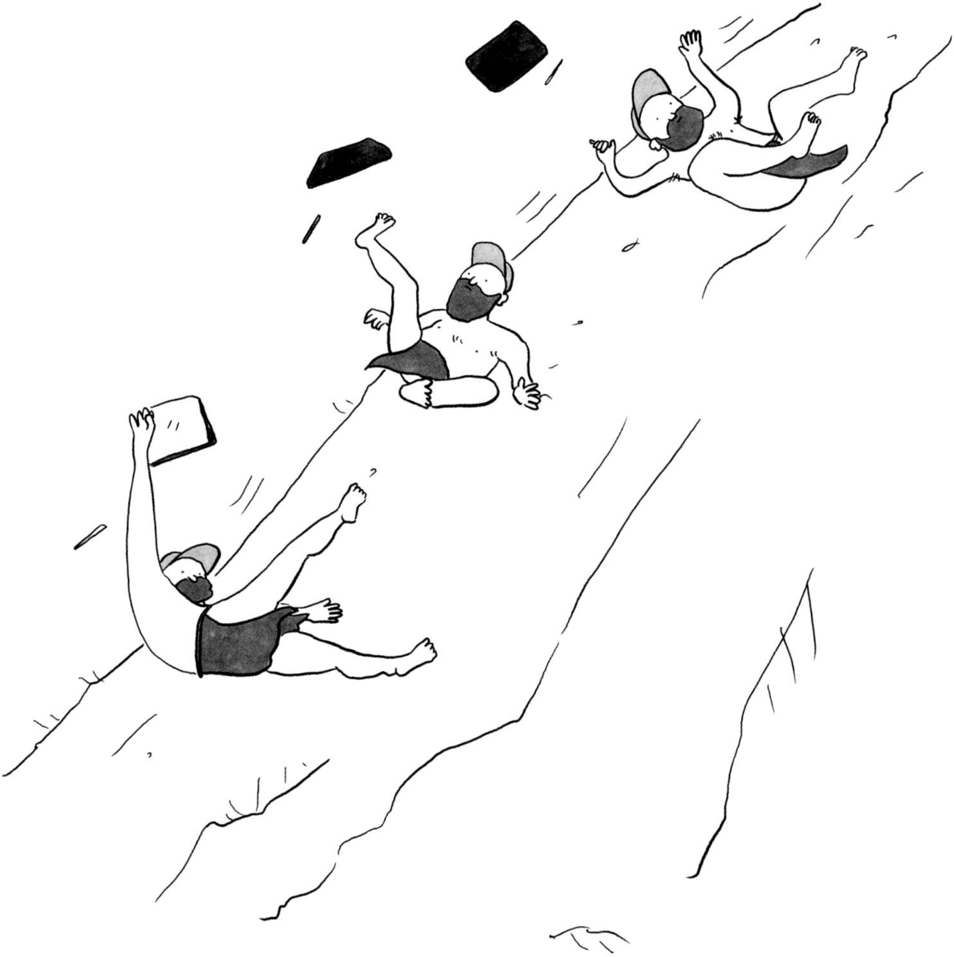

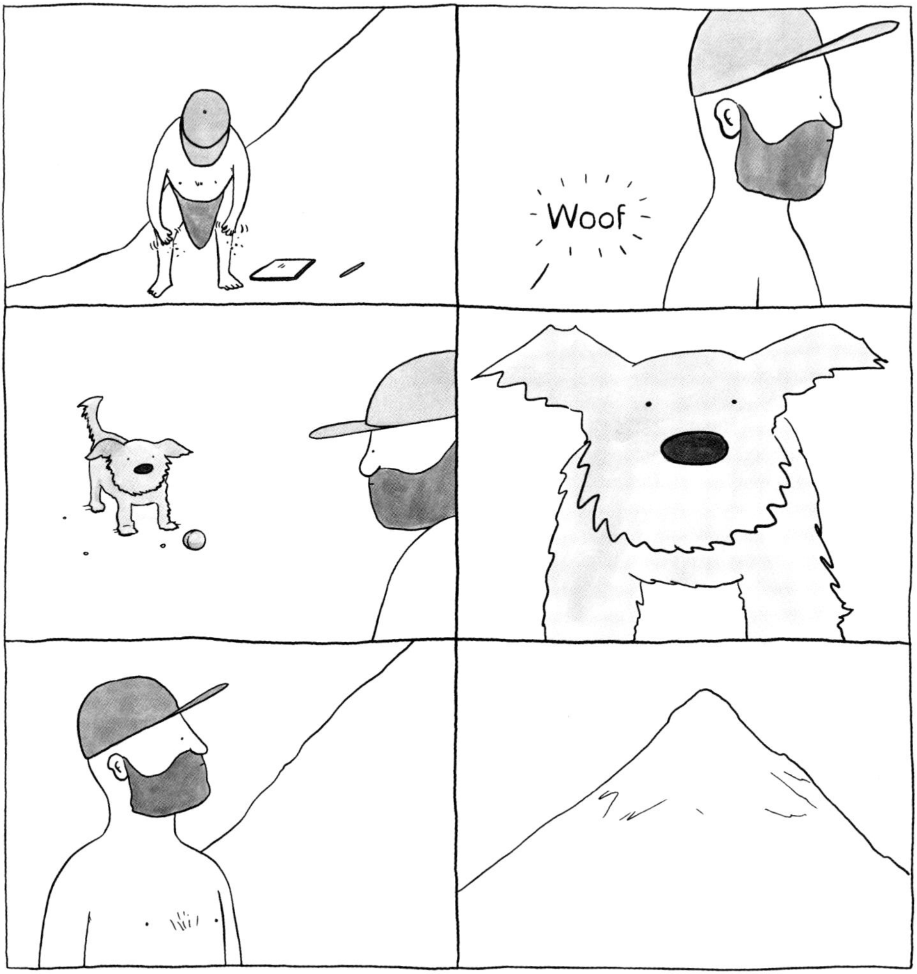
Woof

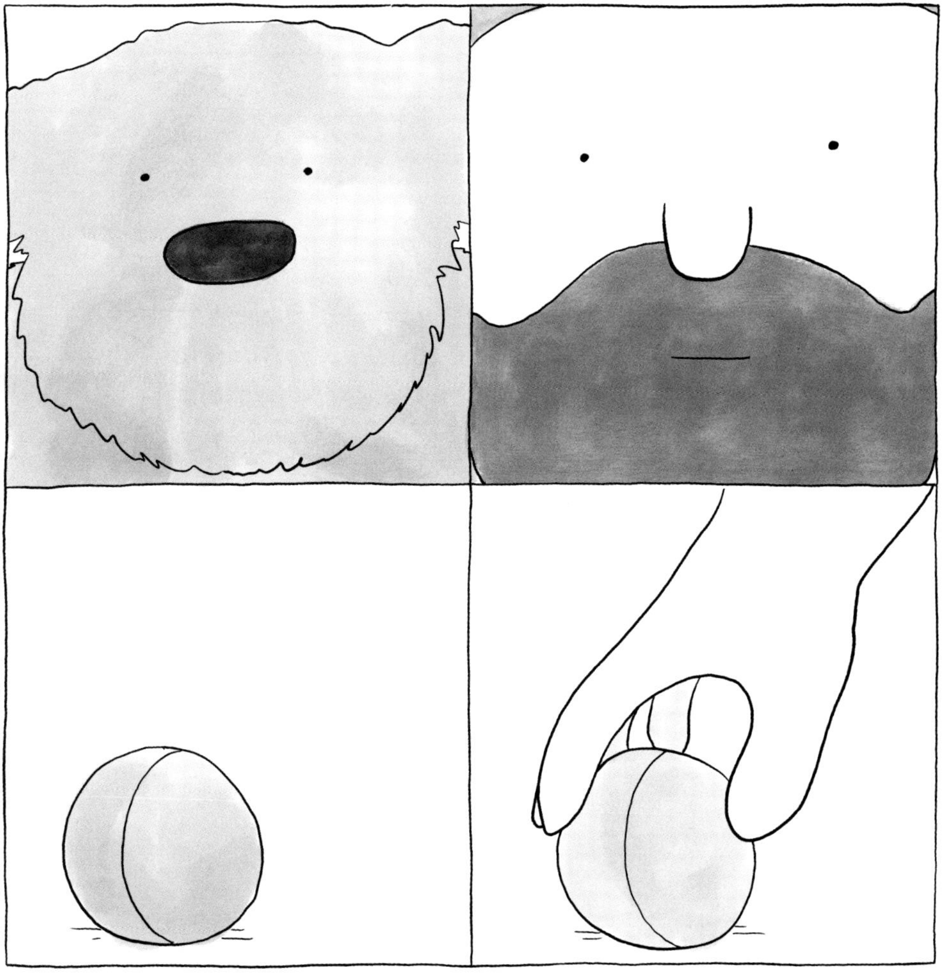

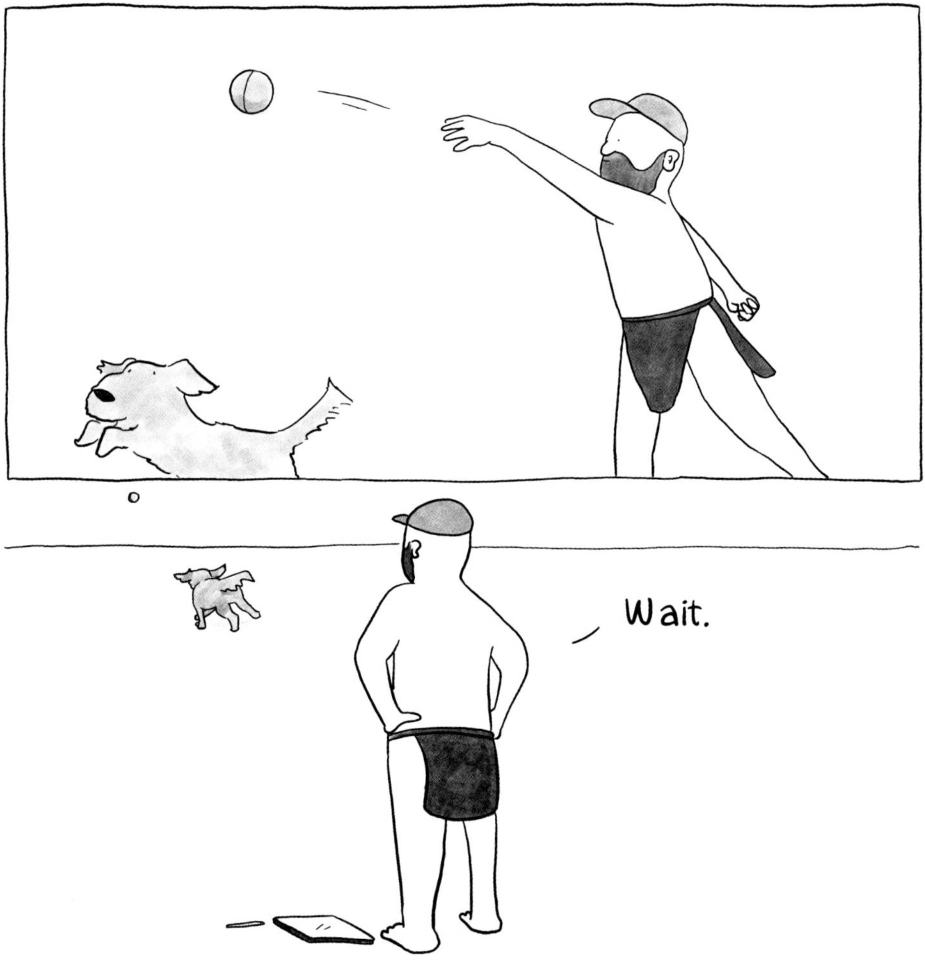
Wait.

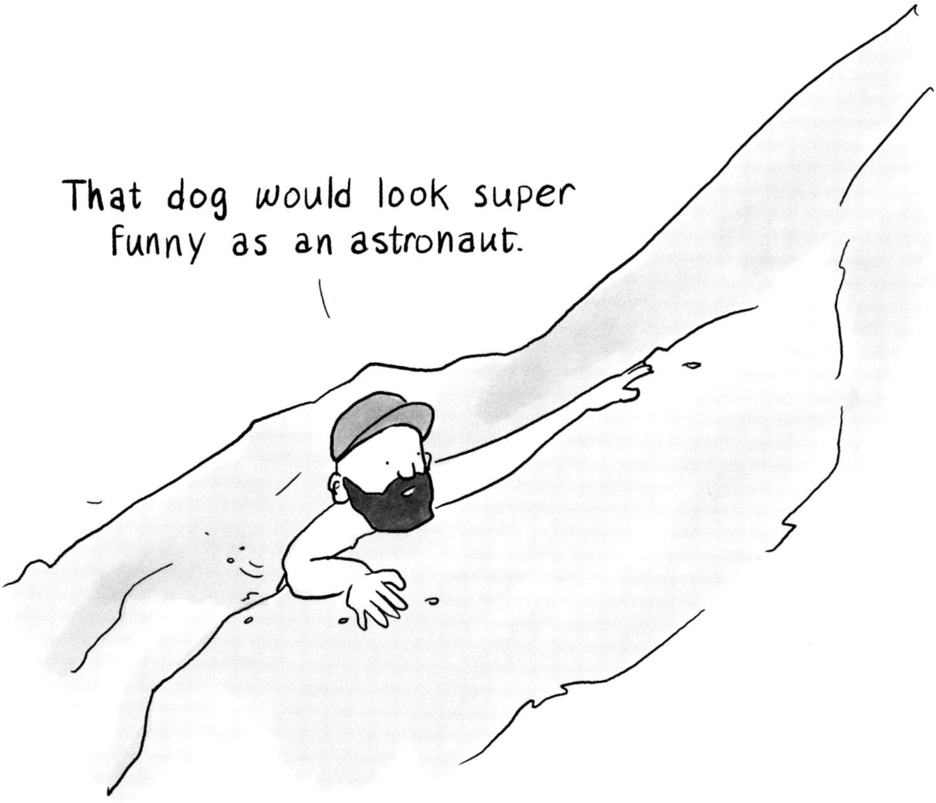
That dog would look super funny as an astronaut.

ACKNOWLEDGMENTS

Thank you, first and foremost, to Nikki Cimoch, whose contributions to this book (and my life) are incalculable.

Additionally, I'd like to acknowledge that nothing I do would be possible without my family: Rachel Perlman, Steve Perlman, Jacob Perlman, Erin Teksten, Reuven Perlman, and Ondrea Perlman. I love you all so much.

Thank you to Patty Rice, Danys Mares, Kat Anstine, Lucas Wetzel, Liz Garcia, Holly Swayne, Chadd Keim, and everyone else at Andrews McMeel.

Thank you to my agents: Julie Flanagan, Jacquie Katz, Andy Elkin, and Ally Shuster.

My gratitude also goes out to the *New Yorker*'s Emma Allen, Rachel Perlman, and David Remnick, and *The Late Show*'s Stephen Colbert and Tom Purcell.

Thank you to Tim Dunn, Steve Waltien, and Eliana Kwartler for helping me with the initial assembly, as well as to my generous friends for giving me feedback throughout the process: River Clegg, Chelsea Davison, Chelsea Devantez, Ariel Dumas, Ivan Ehlers, Django Gold, Lars Kenseth, Andrew Knox, Brendan Loper, Jeremy Nguyen, Vince Portacci, and John Sabine.

Finally, if you should be on this list but are not, I'm sorry, and I have once again omitted the invaluable Ellis Rosen just to make you feel better.